YOU ARE NEERA

SUNIL GANGOPADHYAY was one of India's most well-known writers, writing in Bengali. He wrote novels, poems and children's adventure stories. He was born in Faridpur, which is now in Bangladesh. He studied at the University of Calcutta and earned a master's in Bengali literature. He started a poetry magazine *Krittibas* in 1953 that encouraged young poets. His novels and their translations, *Shei Shomoi* (*Those Days*), *Prothom Alo* (*First Light*), *Moner Manush* (*The Fakir*), among others, have all been best-sellers. He won the Sahitya Akademi Award for *Shei Shomoi*. Many of his novels have been adapted into movies, and two of them have been directed by Satyajit Ray.

One of India's finest translators, ARUNAVA SINHA translates classic, modern and contemporary Bengali fiction and non-fiction into English. Over fifteen of his translations have been published so far, including *Chowringhee* which has sold over 30,000 copies. He was born and grew up in Kolkata, and lives and writes in New Delhi.

YOU ARE NEERA

Sunil Gangopadhyay

Translated by

Arunava Sinha

HARPER PERENNIAL

NEW YORK • LONDON • TORONTO • SYDNEY • NEW DELHI • AUCKLAND

HARPER PERENNIAL

First published in India in 2014 by Harper Perennial
An imprint of HarperCollins *Publishers* India

Building 10, Tower A, 4th Floor, DLF Cyber City, Phase II,
Gurugram Haryana – 122002, India
www.harpercollins.co.in

ISBN: 978-93-5136-155-8

2 4 6 8 10 9 7 5 3 1

Typeset in 11/15 Bell MT at
SURYA

Printed and bound at MicroPrints India, New Delhi

Contents

PREAMBLE

Just for poetry, this life, just for
poetry, this play, just for poetry, alone on a cold day,
traversing the earth, just for poetry
the flash of a tranquil, wide-eyed face
just for poetry are you a woman, just
for poetry so much bloodshed, these cyclonic
depressions
just for poetry am I tempted to live longer,
live a life of regret like human beings, just for poetry
have I disdained immortality.

AN INTRODUCTION

For these verses there is no one else, there's just
    you, Neera
These midnight verses are meant for your private
    intimate face
Waking suddenly from your sleep, pouring yourself
    a glass of water
you will wonder for an instant, biting your tongue,
    who could
be thinking of you at this hour of the night –
    at that moment
every line word syllable of my poetry, with every
    comma dash colon
with every dot on every i, will race towards you,
    in the unruly strands of hair framing your
    half-asleep tender face,
on your bed, these words of mine, silent
    as my breath

Every letter in these verses, like the sorcerer's arrow,
is only meant for you
They know how to pierce only you
Don't be afraid. Sleep. I am a long way away
My dreadful hand will not touch you, this midnight
My impossible arousal, heat, sharp desire and
muffled groan will not terrorize you – my feelings
like the beam of the candle, civilized, cool
on verses of sounds and words
will visit your brow – if they kiss you,
you will not know it; they will lie with you on the
same bed
all night – you will not wake. In the morning
they will droop like dead butterflies near your feet.
Their soul
will merge into every pore of your body, forever.
When I meet you after many years you will laugh
like the waterfall, not knowing any of this.
Neera, I will

gaze at the slanting beauty spot on your lovely face
While I speak of other things I will kiss your radiant
face in my mind
Even in a roomful of people I will look at you
my own way. You will never know – with your
entire body has mingled
the soul of every word in this,
my completely personal poem.

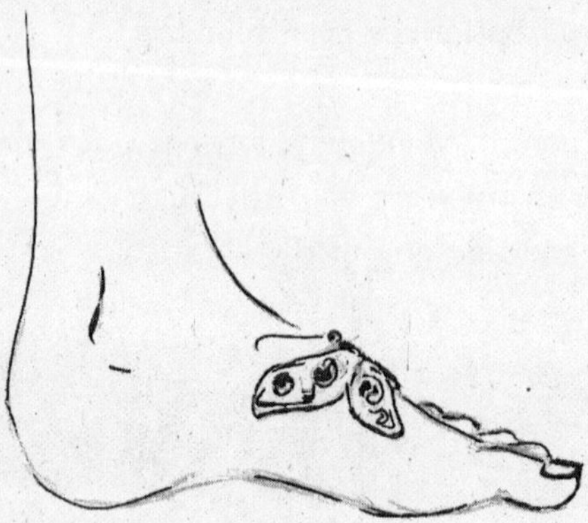

CLOSE TO YOU

Not the morning, but still
the restlessness of first sight
Nor afternoon, and yet
My favourite pastime of the hour
There was no river, but still
I crossed the river to be with you
You weren't there, and yet
It was you I travelled to

Sunlight on the siris trees
Siris? But that's just a desert
Not the evening, but still
Evening hunger and thirst
Fragrant bokul in a letter
A thirst racing to foreign shores
You weren't there, and yet
It was you I travelled to.

FOR NEERA, UNEXPECTEDLY

Three minutes at the bus-stop, yet for hours in my dream last night
I saw you embedded like a knife across the ocean – compass-less –
One body like the fifty-two holy places, in the wind
I saw you last night in my dream, Neera, in the dire blue times
of dreams that ripen once and die.

When did you visit the southern sea-door, with whom?
Have you only just returned?
How terrible, how silent the ocean was in the dream, without a wave,
As though it would kill itself three days later, your horizon in the distance
Like a lost ring, your knees immersed in the blue water

Suddenly you seemed to be a gambler's moll
And yet you were alone, alone in the intense dream.

I shan't sleep for a year, wiping the sweat off the
brow
At dawn after a dream seems so very foolish
I prefer forgetfulness, as free of shame as
The naked body hidden in clothes, I
Shan't sleep for a year, for a year I'll be awake,
dreamless
And roam your body, like the fifty-two holy places,
To earn my piety.

Your smiling face in the bus window. 'I have to go,
come home sometime.'
The shriek of the sunlight drowns all sounds.
'Stay a little longer,' or 'Let's go to the library
garden.'
Someone in my heart said these things,
glancing at my watch with

remembering eyes I jump up, leapfrogging over the
road, buses, trams,
carts and people
Loping on all four limbs like an orang-utan
I reach the door to the office lift.

Three minutes at the bus-stop, yet for hours in my
dream last night.

THERE YOU STAND

There you stand in the balcony
Vanity doesn't become you
Are you just another woman who
from just another balcony
has lain her brow
near evening's head?

For you're mine alone, seen from afar
Dried hair, moist face, your palm cupping your
    silken chin
You are Neera
Vanity simply doesn't become you
To see you is to make you lovely, to become
viewer and god in one
Your solitary beauty merges with the mourning
    wind.

LOOKING

– Are you well?
– Look, clouds. Will it rain?
– Are you well?
– Look, it's dark in the north-west, can you hear the storm?
– Are you well?
– White lightning flashed a moment ago
– Are you well?
– Look at nature
– You're shielding nature
– I'm an atom in a molecule, smaller than the smallest
– You're the one who lights the fire, starts the storm, quickens my blood
– Look, real rain. Look, a real storm.
– I haven't even finished looking at you yet. Are you well?

TO GET

When I touched your hand in the dark
You gave me something, that was all I wanted

Just like visiting the river
Suddenly
Pouring water in cupped hands over my head

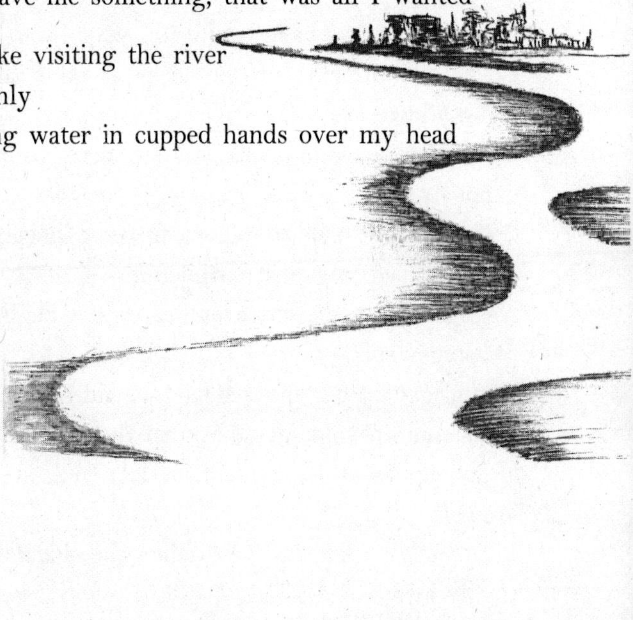

THIS SCENE

Your chin on your knees, you sit there, blue striped
sari
In a dream your hair flowing on your back
Countless butterflies in the air or are they all
skyflowers
Your chin on your knees, you sit there, your eyes
famously distant, a red glow on your toes
On your right hand, the index finger, a smear of ink
You were writing just a while ago
A fragrance in the air, evening prayers begin
somewhere
Night comes from another land, it will be late today
Your chin on your knees, you sit there, in the veins
of art there's an excitement, in art's eyes are
fireworks
Like restless glances, like fireflies, the charming lies
fly away

I cannot even remember I was unhappy once
Your chin on your knees, you sit there, time does
not stop
I know, one day death will come and take me away
across the horizon
New men will appear, build a new society
A new breeze will wipe out the old breaths
But still, today
Your chin on your knees, you sit there, this pose
These locks of flowing hair on your back
The smear of ink on your finger
This scene is forever, immortality will make friends
with it
Your chin on your knees, you sit there

NEGLECTED BY POETRY

Just a girl, nothing more, facing the mirror, doing
her hair
Why are men so charmed by this, do the girls even
know?
For even the men comb their hair, shave and shower,
swim and play
Must all this be only prose? What does it mean?
Will girls never know?

NEAR YOU, NEERA

Who were those people speaking quietly on the
staircase?
They left, shutting the door, and still you stood on
the steps
Your hands and chin on the railing, no one would
think you're stilled lightning
Your complexion is a little dark, as though stolen
from a lotus leaf
You remained standing
I was suddenly reminded of Neera
when I saw you, Neera

I see you just two days a year, Neera
On Holi and on Saraswati Puja – both amidst colours
Just two days amongst colours and flowers
You're different on those two days,
you're a different Neera

Other sentries surround you the other three sixty-
three days

You haven't seen me in a secluded room, I have
hidden
my wantonness from you, none of us has ever joined
our palms
at our chests to touch emptiness, ever spoken to
each other
Near our breasts, ever circled the fragrance of one
another's eyes
I have hidden my wantonness
From you, Neera, I see you only two days a year

I was suddenly reminded of Neera
when I saw you, Neera
I did not desire you, I did not try to reel you in
I did not enter your temple-like body
on trumped-up excuses
I did not annihilate you casually with a blood-
smeared hand

I meet you on Holi and Saraswati Puja – you stood
near the stairs today in such a new way
Neera, I shall be forever indebted to you for Neera.

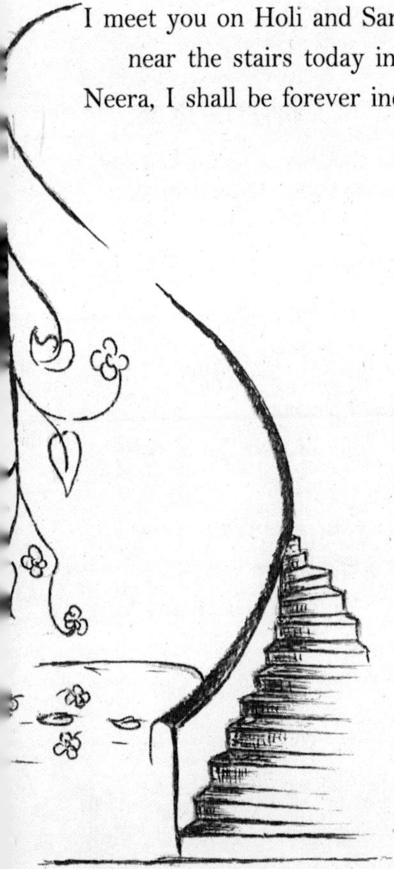

SEEING NEERA

I cannot bear distances, Neera, come close to me like the night of a thunderstorm
Just as the cannonballs of summer mourn on the riverbed
As impatient as every silk-cotton tree bathed in fire
I wait

With a shawl of rain and on light feet, like a bride, sit for a minute in the veranda
The light on one side of your face, diffused on the other, a radiant black
What are those grains on your eyebrows, what the elusive sport of your soft fingers
Let me look at you closely, I've hardly seen anything in this ordinary life

This shamelessly physical man has not yet touched
the roots of your stillness
Look, on the swan feather
In his hand is written spring exile.

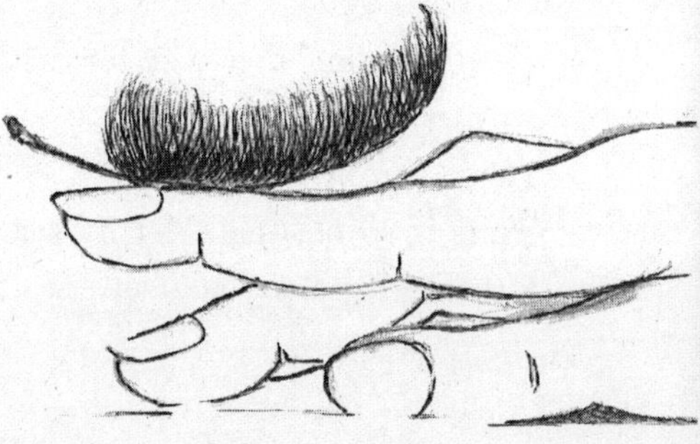

NEERA AT THAT MOMENT

Your magnolia feet on grass wet with dew
Looking into your eyes are the eyes of
    freshly bloomed jasmines
At that moment, Neera, you didn't even realize
that the bee abandoned the flower and said,
Let me touch the girl

You were a woman, what good deed made you a girl
    again?
On the riverbank you scattered naked excesses
Can even eternity halt, even time lose its way?
Your eyes hold memories of heaven
Your lips, immortality

Keep standing that way for a while, Neera,
so that you seem unreal
Don't vanish
Time is so obstinate, let its soldiers
kneel and grasp your feet.

NEAR NEERA

The moment you opened the door I turned from
beast to man
A tornado played over my body, a yellow joy
Instead of opening the door, you could have said the
time was wrong
You didn't, your mercy made the day golden, flowers
showered on my desire

You live impossibly far away now,
take this distance further
Neera, don't you remember the scene
by heaven's river?
In a jasmine necklace the breeze takes wing alone in
the afternoon
All the mangy, homeless dogs on the street are my
companions now

I'll hold your thirsty face on my breast, warm breath touching my heart
Is this simple wish an indulgence, not a square meal for the famished?
Deprived of this, he will eat inedible scraps, mourn on the pier
Don't you remember the demon breaking down the door at midnight?

A blast of golden colour seemed to flow out of oblivion
The moment you opened the door I turned from beast to man.

COME, LET'S…

Come, let's talk in that language which
No one will understand
Neither you, nor me
Come, let's exchange dreams
Dreams that I haven't had yet
Nor have you

Come, let's scatter around the garden
Seeds of flowers never seen
Even though we have no garden of our own

Some people are coming our way, beating war drums
A river ran dry a minute ago
New fences are coming up on the border
The guards are laughing
This one in a cage, that one too
Even the prisoners clap
Some people are coming our way, beating war drums

Come, let's start a worldwide festival of destruction
The kind of destruction even the world has never seen.

WHAT I WANTED, WHAT I WON'T GET

– What do you want from me?
– I didn't ask for anything, did I?
– That's true. Then why do you
 call out to me like a storm?
– I don't know. Look, there's the water
 Like silver in the sunlight
 Like your eyes
 The distant boat
 It's you I see everywhere
– Tell me truly, poet, what do you want from me?
– I think you're a goddess…
– I'm no goddess.
– But you don't know who you are.
– Who am I?
– You are Saraswati, and since the word originally meant
 female, you are within reach
 Sometimes I call you woman

– You make me laugh. You always say
whatever comes to mind, don't you?
– Most of the time. Whatever comes to mind...
Why does it come to mind?
– What do you want, tell me truly. Don't change the subject.
– Blessings.
– Blessings? Mine, or the real goddess's?
– You are she. Across the table
The pale red sari
Fingers touching the chin
Come to me
Bless me, put your hand on my head
Drive me mad with your blessings
Clutch my hair, draw blood
From my brow with your nails
– You're mad enough. You want to be madder still?
– Only when I see you. Or else I'm tranquil
– Then it's best to not see me, isn't it?

– If I had spent my life caring for what's best
and what's not,
it would have been a lark's life, a robin's
or a wild cat's or Mahatma Gandhi's
or the life of a worm in rice stalks
– What about a human life?
– Do you think I'm human? I was, though
before I saw you
– You look straight into my eyes
You gaze for a long time
You don't even blink
What do you see?
– The you within you, when you take off your
clothes and ornaments
You
The you behind all of those
– Is that really me? Or your imagination?
– Look, little girl…
– You just called me a goddess

– Same thing. The vessel of imagination is the
 goddess –
 You are that Neera
 I need your blessings
– That's not very difficult. I can give it at once.
– You have so much, give me a drop
– What do I have? I don't know
– You are, you are, there's no greater truth
– We met on the stairs
 You didn't say anything then.
 My lonely days, my unseasonal ways
 Are all mine – only the breeze from my
 childhood knows
– Will you give me a fraction of your sorrows? I
 shall be enriched
– I have no sorrows – even more than sadness
 A noble raptness
 has gathered around me
 It can't be shared
 What else do I have that I can give you?

– You are, you are, there's no greater truth
You're a goddess, I want to kneel
With your palm on my head, blessings
But it doesn't end there
Not a poet, I turn into a male in a flash
My restless hands
want to grasp with all ten fingers
your waist like a lioness's
Like a baby rubs its face on your body
As though fidgeting to learn a secret
– Go away, male, come closer, poet
What can I give you?
– Nothing
– Hurt?
– Call it hurt
– This is nice! What if
I name the illness exile
Not seeing you, non-existence
And distance, hurt?

– How much distance, after all? You remember?
– How did you think I could forget?
– You sitting here, your fingertips touching your chin
Strands of hair on your forehead
Your feet hidden by the pattern on the edges
An imminent smile on the corners of your lips
Immortality lies in this scene
You have no idea, Neera,
The image will remain even after my death
– Will time stay still? What do you want from me?
– Death?
– No, don't say that
– Then affection? I'm such a beggar for affection
– Haven't you got it?
– I can't quite tell. When an elderly man wants affection

He wants the body too
Can you press your cheeks to his to give
him a sweet warmth?
– Madness once more?
– Show yourself
– I want to see you too
– No
– Why not?
– Don't say that. Don't say that ever again
It frightens me
This is one-sided
Who am I? Insignificant, ordinary, a
nobody
But still I dare your beauty
– You're a poet?
– Do you think I remember? I keep forgetting
I turn obstinate, seeking favours
– What do you want from me?
– Nothing. If there's a speck in my eyes
will you remove it with your warm breath?

A FRAGMENT

– Who goes there?
– Overwhelmed, night just left
– What is that sound nearby?
– The shadow returning from the sunlight
– Has the torrent returned where it was
    supposed to?
– The moon has forgotten her, has it?
– What is that scent in the air?
– I kissed a swan
– Has anyone come to claim a debt?
– Someone who had wept for you
    Who placed, on your arm,
    a repentant face
– Who goes there?
– The wind was here
– What is that sound nearby?
– A flower falling to earth
    A fresh flower blossoming

– Has the moon returned
from the other side of oblivion?
– The torrent has taken her away
– What is that scent in the air?
– The thick blood of a swan pierced by an arrow
– Has anyone become free of debt?
– You were not born blind, not mute, not deaf
Why all these questions still?
– Born under an impatient star, I keep coming back
Holding an unfulfilled vessel
to your eyes, Neera

POETRY PERSONIFIED

She's on the bed, her open blue notebook in front
The woman lies face down, her feet beyond the edge
Wet hair on her back
And a pair of waves in the sea
A fragrance in the room full of shade
Says that
Sunlight is a droplet of water,
    a distant land of blue stars
What does she write? Poetry? Or does poetry
    compose her?
She's too restless, her eyes hold too many tears
Her face in profile
is stillness personified
The careless sari shows
    the naked veranda at the waist
With a mountain scene
A green, fresh valley

Why isn't she a river? Or is she celestial
What does she write? Poetry? Or does poetry
    compose her?
Sudden rain in the city, the afternoon is flooded
She hasn't seen it, hasn't heard a sound
As though an island
where a shade of yellow invites crimson
Or she's a mermaid
Diamond scales on her arms
The quill in her fingers brightening like a picture
What does she write? Poetry? Or does poetry
    compose her?

ON THE STAIRCASE

There was no room anywhere, you asked me to
    sit on the stairs

You were about to sweep the dust with the end of
    your sari, I said, never mind
I had wanted to wipe the sweat on my face with that
    part of your sari
But it remained billowing between us
like the sword in the proverb
over which blows
a sensitive wind
Footsteps broke the silence of the staircase every
    now and then
I sit, shrinking back, why can't willpower enable a
    man to be invisible at will
Pinning unfamiliar glances on my body,
    Neera, you laugh

Your intangible laughter turns the stairs into the
edge of a waterfall
Over which a loving tree bends
The reflections of the leaves play in the water
New eyelashes, a new pensive invitation
My desire is so distant from your tender stability
Still the pain of long separation turned to dust on
the staircase

TALKING

I see you, I do not find a way to talk to you
I see you in the soft morning breeze, in the powdery
    light of the late afternoon
At the crossroad you were rushing about for a taxi
    in the rain, Neera
I was at the window of a passing tram
You came out of the French film festival as a
    deity of happiness
I was getting my torn slippers repaired by the cobbler
Climbing to the top of the Monument, you beckoned
    to me
I had to race down the stairs to the Underground
We came face to face one day, remember?
Fires were raging across the entire city
Everyone was screaming, in unfamiliar voices
One mustn't talk at such times,
    words become bankrupt

Poetry is marred by words used wrongly
Like the mistaken sound of butterflies being singed
by the fire,
love burns
An unsaid thing or two remain glowing like a lapis
lazuli
in the breast

THE FIRST QUESTION

When I was a lump of flesh without nails and teeth
    in my mother's womb
I had a dream in which
A woman named Neera stood by a river, the end of
    her sari
fluttering in the wind like heaven's own flag
A young man stood in front of her,
    leaning on a sword
The scene shimmered, cutting through the darkness.
Then I was born on a night when lightning flashed
Someone smeared honey on my lips, sprinkled
    rosewater on my eyes
I didn't want all these intolerable excesses,
    where was Neera, where was the woman

Many years have passed since then, the dream
did not prove entirely untrue
Sometimes I see Neera, not just by the river
Neera walks at the edge of the valley
But who was the young man? I cannot
find him, but I keep looking, looking.

A PLEA

Don't you send a storm to the lovely woman's home,
 sky

Let the tremulous beam of the lamp keep quivering
Let her spread the end of her sari on the floor, press
 her breasts to it
Waiting alone in her room, the apple of the eye of
 the heavens

Her body like a lagoon is filled with soft water
Though marks of pain are drawn by her coward
 lover
The trader's servant, dead afraid to be alive

Still don't send a storm, sky, to the home of the
 lovelorn woman

Let her stay with her breasts pressed to her sari
 spread out on the floor

Let the tremulous beam of the lamp glimmer as it quivers
So that the lover can put it out with a swift puff of his breath.

EVERY TIME THE FIRST MEETING

Neera's handwritten letter came
    as the light was dying
I was snarled in the coils of a knotted thread
Amidst all this a freshly bathed magnolia
Like a drowning man gasping for breath
I too told the sun, take your time today
Neera has asked for me, don't blur, horizon
What's this rattling on the window,
    calm down, latch
Keep waiting, page that the book's open at
Ink stain on the finger, be a darling and disappear
Smiling like a newborn waterfall,
    the magnolia looked on,
Every time I meet Neera for the first time
    it's by a waterfall
A sunbeam has broken through the cloud to fall on
    the line of her chin

The light in her eyes is like the leaf of a fresh tree
 in spring
Bobbing on her breast,
 a young boy swims in the ocean
Neera has asked for me,
 vanish in the wilderness, cloud
Someone else has come to the door,
 I'm nowhere to be seen
Stop, sound, be silent, speech
I must snap these coils of thread and stand up
I have to go, I have to go…

HUMILIATION AND A RESPONSE TO NEERA

Why did you laugh on the stairs,
three friends stood witness
Why did you laugh on the stairs,
three friends stood witness
Why did you laugh on the stairs, Neera, why did you laugh, why
Like a clap of thunder in my sleep, as though you stood on the stairs
Stood on the stairs and laughed, Neera,
three friends stood witness
On the stairs why the laughter why the witnesses why friends why three why
Why did you laugh on the stairs,
three friends stood witness

I touched your hand once, seven or eleven months later that hand
A little thinner, neither cold nor warm, more miraculous than the past

Blood pounding like laughter,
    that hand belongs to me
If I hadn't held a cigarette I'd have wrapped mine
    around it and smelt it
If I hadn't held a cigarette I'd have wrapped mine
    around it and smelt it
Not the face or the hair, I understand everything
    when I touch that hand, I
Am greater than all the doctors of the world, I have
    touched your hand
And found the sound of a distant bee, echoed by the
    emptiness of the flower

Of the flower? Or of crops? The train whistles
    beneath the balcony
Like a joke
Tickets have been bought, going abroad again, to
    the sea or the river
Abroad again
That hand will wave a handkerchief
    from the train window

Down in the street it's not cold,
    my breath is light, quick
The taxi races to heaven, loud laughter floats in the
    magic night
Not a bit of fog in my head,
    a lovely half-sleep in my eyes
Sleep! I remember sleep, you, sleep, sleep, you, sleep,
    why sleep on the stairs
Do you bathe before you sleep? You seemed to in my
    dream, Neera...

Or sing? The bathroom mirror brings dreadful
    memories, do you remember,
The bus-stop? In a dream within a dream – in a
    dream, at the bus-stop
We never met there, it was just poetry.
    My sadness today
And yet what sadness, the profuse sorrows of sadness,
    poor thing
Sadness possesses man like a spirit,
    no sadness at the crossroads, Neera

Unlocking my heart some of my sadness unlocking my chest, if it could be
Touched with the hand, with the hand, then another poem in the
grey notebook, or the sadness of no sorrows … love isn't greater than this.

RIGHT NEXT TO LOVE

An illness lies right next to love
How can I ask it to go?
Won't it follow civilized norms?
It catches my eye every now and then,
  makes me tremble
An illness lies right next to love

Like the flickering of the flame, shielded
by cupped hands, you're my secret
There's envy in there too, a sharp point
Like a diacritical
Obstinate like in childhood
I look around but the heart won't listen
An illness lies right next to love

I kiss you, tumble at your feet
Put you on a throne and play with fire
Still my own heart burns, my heart burns
My heart burns
No one understands

An illness lies right next to love.

LOVE

Isn't love those teeth marks on the breast?
Is love just the longing in the rain?
So love is the heat from a heart close by?
Love means the tiger has tasted blood

Love was alone by the waterfall
Without a bridge to walk across the sky
Love was being the golden corn on the field
Love was sunlight on the railway tracks

Body spent, chest covered in sweat
Arm on head, sleep comes in waves
In my sleep I say over and over
I shall give my love to love itself.

NEERA, YOU...

Neera, you just gave a fistful of rice to the starving
Won't you give me some?
I sleep on the burning-grounds, eat ash, roll in it
My days pass copulating with the river
This river saw Gautama Buddha
Smeared itself with gunpowder later
You, this river

It's very late, the sky will soon be dressed
Dense blossoms in the bamboo grove of the century
Haven't you heard the thudding drumbeats?
Resurrected water speaks from the depths
Deserts and poles beckon to one another
Listen, go to the corridors of the heart and listen
Raise your glittering finger, cherished illusionist,
Not in poetry, not in the body of the river – take
your glasses off and wash your face in rainwater,
    Neera
And bring it close
Neera, come to me as Neera.

SILVER WOMAN

Silver woman, don't let the July rain this evening
drench your face, your silver eyes.
    Come up to the veranda, instead.
Wicker chairs inside, doors closed, windows closed
Unlock them, silver woman,
    press the switch on the wall
or sit in the dark, let the windowpanes stay shut
See the rain from afar today,
    wicker chairs in the room,
Unlock the door.
No keys? What! Search your handbag carefully,
    your heart or the carpet beneath your feet,
    lift the corners and look
Check the letterbox, silver woman, why is it taking
    so long?
Rain outside, torrential rain,
    gusts of wind wrap themselves

around you, untying your silver hair, find the key
Your silver helpless face makes me even more eager
Hammer on the door! Maybe it'll open on its own,
    the lock is flimsy
Being such a restless silver woman doesn't suit you
Or because it is alone, the rain cannot touch you by
    hook or by crook.
You won't step back into the blazing storm
Unlock the door.
Silver woman, sit in the wicker chair
    by the window today
Alone in these darknesses or switch the light on
Put your silver face on the cool windowpane,
    open your eager eyes wide
Rain outside, torrential rain, today with your silver
    body
You'll see rain cover the earth, currents wrung out
    of the sky

I'm standing beneath a rain in the distance,
    standing alone
All my body is drenched, my body of steel, let it be
    drenched today
Standing alone I don't believe in thunder or lightning,
    all day long
I gaze at that window piercingly,
    on this side of the glass
No matter how much the wind strikes, still your
    silver eyes
Today, drenched alone in the rain, silver woman, I
    shall watch
You sitting alone not getting drenched in the rain

IN THE AFTERNOON

There's a thorny bush by your face, shift a little
A wall this side, so many cobwebs
On the other side, a river, or is it envy?
In truth a shadow is cast on the busy afternoon by
    childhood love
There are no men in the crowd of men
Overwhelmed adolescence at the impossibly
    desolate crossroads
Wavering footsteps, you came after such a long time?
There's a thorny bush by your face, shift a little

ONE OR TWO WISHES

One or two wishes just won't let me go
I was set to leave by the nine-thirty train
All arrangements made, nightsuit buttoned up
A heaven lying just beyond these three lighthouses
One or two wishes just won't let me go

In play we met and when we stopped
    it was late at night
Clinging to my body was a distance-driven breeze
A woman's scent like a river, a memory of a trance
All of it near my heart, as near as the sky
One or two wishes still won't let me go

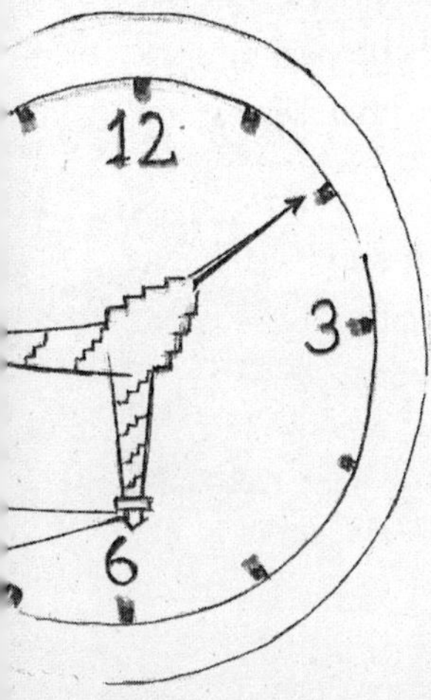

NEERA'S ILLNESS

When Neera is ill, everyone in Kolkata feels low
After sunset, before they start glowing, the neon
    lights ask suddenly,
Is Neera well today?
The ancient church clock, the scarlet grace of the
    store – they know
Neera is well today.
In offices, cinemas, parks, through the lips of millions
    of people spreads news of Neera.
The sharp smell of fragrant flowers arrives to say
    Neera is happy today
When the apathetic wind suddenly prances all over
    the sky, sending a thousand bells pealing
All the people of Kolkata smile to themselves, for
    Neera has emerged today.

When the sky is overcast, when sorrow soars over
    the sultry, shadow-encrusted city,

When a taxi pierces the belly of a tram, causing a
joyless traffic jam at the crossroads,
When in restaurants and on roads everyone's face is
like thunder, wearing masks of annoyance
When anger and strikes overrun Kolkata, when the
rioting is about to begin
When people will burn down telephone- and post-
offices
When their heartbeats will go on strike, too...
Knowing, shuddering with fear, I run instantly to
Neera to ask her,
Are you melancholy, Neera?
Darling girl, look at me but once, show me the
bough of your face as to a mirror
Let me hear you laugh like a fresh stream as you
answer my riddle!
Instantly, the veil is lifted, it starts raining, people
go to watch movies and football matches with
contented faces

The traffic is unsnarled, the tempo and the cycle, the rickshaw and the car, all wend their separate ways home together
With cigarettes dangling from their lips some people say, life's not too bad.

A FOREIGN LAND

One look at your lips and I know you're a traveller
    in our land
That neck, the arch of those brows,
    don't belong here
That mottled light on the crown, that look you flash
That face, that cleavage, they don't belong here.

In the post-rain afternoon,
    the roads are full of dry mud
All of us are distressed, our hearts turned to stone
Your feet did not touch the ground
Your smile only comparable to a bird
Let it rain again, you said.

All of us wanted beauty
Wanted justice, money, sex
Your hands only held sand
Like a harsh day, our discontent is full of harshness

One fire lights another, flames flow from the eyes
Spotting the empty harvest in the wind
    you clapped

This earth is a foreign land to you
How long will you stay?
You're travelling, is that why your face is tinged
    with joy?
If I capture you
Hold the buzzing bee in my fist
Will the wrath of the gods vaporize me?

THE SHADOW

Don't you stand opposite Neera, Hiranmay
I don't like it.
Don't you stand by her side, I don't like it.
You may caress Neera's shadow.
You have no divine spark, Hiranmay, your shirt is
missing a button, your dagger, its handle.
So much sweat on your body, joy in your blood,
restless eyes
Why are you in the guise of a killer?
Being a killer doesn't suit you.
You'd better be a lover.
Don't you stand in front of her, or by her side.
You may kiss the mouth of Neera's shadow.

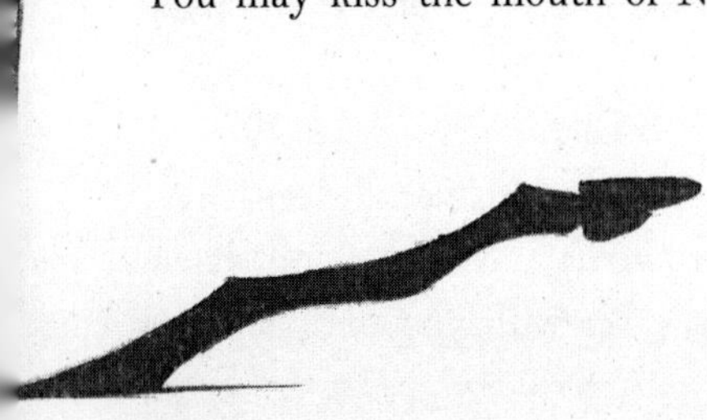

PLAYED MANY SPRINGS

We've played many springs but we still have
an unfinished kiss
I'm sitting alone by the river as dusk falls
No, incorrect, I haven't seen a river like this
in a long time
Written in a burst of poetry, like a beloved image
Can't I write it without having seen it? Aren't
images as real as art?
Never mind all that now, I know a secluded river
is waiting for me somewhere

Like the marvellous trip to the Valley of Flowers
that year
No, I didn't snap a single branch, didn't even clamp
my teeth
on anyone's breasts
But still the fragrant bed robbed me of sleep
Remember the golden evening, Neera? I still have
one night's sleep with you unfinished.

AFTER LIVING ABROAD

Take my hand, Jamuna, we're going to heaven
Come, lock your mouth, your eyes,
    your body, with mine
Come as pure as a fresh leaf
Heaven isn't very far,
    like the voices that waft in from
the North Sea when spring is in exile, like the
    warmth of winter
from the arm that owes a debt to another's breasts.
    Take my hand, Jamuna, we're going to heaven.

My time abroad ended today, such a sweet parting
man has never known. Jamuna is my companion – a
    thousand handkerchiefs
wave towards heaven, Jamuna, I ensure you're a
    close neighbour to the constellations
Are you actually not the legendary tears of the star
    named Swati?

Are you not the moonlit night in the fragrance of
the lime leaf left behind?
Are you not a slender stick of incense?
You're no one
You're oblivion, you're made of sounds, the colour of
woman, in your breasts and thighs
You are woman
In travel and in rest you are the thirst for love in
every book
Woman to trusting eyes, in sweat and hair, in the
dirt under cracked nails
In every molecule you are woman, woman within
woman, beauty laughing in emptiness
You are the heretic Manisha's taunt,
every young poet's
Neera, touching your sweetness through
error and sleep,
All the rants and angry greed become river currents
Because you kiss sinners,
the sentries unlock heaven's gates

Is this what you're like? You're no one
except my Jamuna.
Take my hand,
    let us add the rhythm of dance to descriptions
of embarrassed scenes from life, come, take my hand.
I have suffered too much on this earth, in distrust
I am a murderer, I am a cheat in the underground
    city, a fugitive
in the forest, a debtor at the meat shop,
    I disrupt celebrations as a spy in disguise!
But despite my doubts I have not forgotten the way
    to paradise, like my former homeland
You know nothing, neither love nor a low-hung
    heaven, which is just as well
You are the adolescent river, the currents of
    forgetfulness, the reward of evening…

Come, little girl,
    let's play in the garden of heaven today.

THREE SHADOWS NEXT TO NEERA

Neera and three shadows next to Neera
I've strung an arrow on the bow, but the shadows
    are so shameless
they won't leave her alone
Now the bow's drawn back, I'll fire the arrow like a
    storm
Raising her arms, Neera said, 'You shan't, hunter!
I know them so well!'
The grief in my breast swirls with the whirling dust
Neera smiled in mock severity,
    with her the proud shadows
The returned arrow glanced off my eyes
Neera doesn't know.

A BUNDLE OF UNGRATEFUL WORDS

Today, the regret of unwritten letters tingles
on my fingers or eyelids
In the afternoon near New Market unexpectedly I
forget Neera's surname
and Neera's face
The way drowning men gasp for breath –
the same anxiety
The image of Neera's face – gold-rimmed glasses?
Or black?
A slanted beauty spot on an arched brow, the breeze
flirting with flowing hair
Still Neera's face is indistinct, misty
Summoning the fenced-in bokul tree, I ask
You saw her too, didn't you?
Are Neera's glasses gold-rimmed or black?

Like a flight of steps, loss of memory descends a
long way
I forget the smell of Neera's navel

The amused sadness in her eyes
Was there a mole on Neera's chin?
The cardamom-flavoured laughter is like mockery in
 the wind
In my oblivion I hear the dense sound of downfall
In the afternoon near New Market, unexpectedly
My existence, in the process of forgetting it all,
 is emptied out but rapt
The blue curtains are ripped apart, innumerable
 walls crumble
The shadow of a forest of oaks plays
 next to the clouds
The bundle of ungrateful words rings out sharply
At that very moment, my jaws clenched, I raise my
 hand, a death grip
A bloodied dagger flashes...

EXILE

Nikhilesh and I, that is, I and Nikhilesh, that is, the
four of us
Together in the evening
Walk though Curzon Park – princess lights all
around us
The insurance company's clock makes us fearful
as its hands run backwards, our figures have bent
heads, the four of us walk by,
cigarettes change places
on our lips, we don't talk, from the multihued flower
gardens on either side of Red Road coloured winds
blow, like
magic with cards the cars come and go,
what matches this
is the breath of a dying river, we walk on, we had
been to a
broken-down factory to buy chains,
we're returning, I

look at the other three and they, at me,
sidelong glances
In bright and dim lights our shadows are equidistant
Twisting my ankle in a rathole or wormhole on the
moonlit field
I drop back, they don't notice, they walk on
Sometimes they're in the light, sometimes in the
shade beneath trees
They don't turn back, they don't stop, they go on…
I call out to my shadow in an atheist's voice, a
hundred girls' screams,
plus laughter, rise thrice next to the Memorial
shielding it, this time I shout my name out very loud
Before anyone can answer, an auctioneer bangs his
gavel, as I
am about to throw a stone, someone asks,
'Sunil, what are you doing here?'
Wiping the blood on my knee and brow

on the grass I see at once trembling reds and greens
    in the dark
I want to raise my arms upwards to shield myself
    from the judging eyes of
the Great Bear. 'Get up, come home, or tell us
where you have hidden Neera.' A man cannot be
    recognized from
his voice, a blind girl had once told me,
    I urge my eyes
to investigate the man; who can walk down the
    path where
there's no sin, no sorrow? As though a hunter had
    arrived after
traversing a dense forest,
    the sharpest question of life
on his lips, he stood, touching with fingers like
    temple spires
a blue emptiness – as though so familiar, yet the face
    is not,

nor the eyes, so heartless the man had no shadow,
    a lifetime's sorrows rose in my breast.
'Where have you hidden her?' 'I don't know.'
The words
like blood on the brow, but still they don't understand
    the language of blood
Thirst and failure keep asking. I don't know where
    I have hidden Neera, or
where Neera has hidden me. Where was Nikhilesh
    lost, in existence
The shadow and the figure, each other… I kept
    walking alone again for a long time
No one came along – not the question, not the
    shadow, not Nikhilesh, not love
Only exile

THE AMORPHOUS KINGDOM

In my mother's rose bush a flower just like a rose
has bloomed
I see it with eyes like eyes, at dawn like dawn
a pure flame is lit on the matchstick, with a cigarette
    in my lips
I descend from the roof to the principal earth
Moist grass beneath my feet, just beneath my feet
    moist grass

When a man wakes up with sadness, sadness stays
    awake, the man sleeps again
On the sentry's perturbed knees
Not a man, but I. My sleepwalking considers the
    recent breeze
The wind of the century
And the woman, a dream. Not a woman, but Neera.
Her glance turns to a sunbird and flies off.
    The dream

is the fragrance of jasmine on her breast. The dream
makes Neera's flowing laughter sound like a lustrous
waterfall. Also a dream –
the sunbird, the jasmine, the waterfall – all of them
flower as
the infinite harvest of this dusty earth
Just as Neera is the harvest. Me. In sadness
everything is a dream.

Envy is a sleeping position. Coming close to the
woman's or Neera's body
it rattles like a chain
My eyes turn to pointed daggers,
the palace towers collapse
The platform of politics destroys,
transformation begins
Man appears a water-beast, minor feminine organs
are like food
Love is salt and pepper, fire in its breath
Every dawn is like daybreak, like a razor-blade the
sun turns into

a flowering virgin, clouds into dire times –
all dreams!
Sometimes I wake up when the sleep of sadness
starts, sensing which way the wind is blowing
With eyes exactly like eyes
Taking a drag on my cigarette I laugh raspingly
Living is like this
I am a citizen of this amorphous kingdom
In the rose seed, just like a blooming rose, the very
own glow of the visible harvest
Moist grass beneath the feet, only beneath the feet
wet grass

WHICH BANK ARE YOU ON, NEERA?

Which bank are you on, Neera, I'm in the middle of
the river
The clouds lean, closing in on us
Like innumerable handkerchiefs, blue, black
darkness comes, swaying on the petals of the sun
In the sudden wind even a few homebound birds
lose the day
Which bank are you on, Neera, I'm in the middle of
the river

Masses of people on the deck of the ferry
None of them has seen me
I'm no one in the ferry world
They only give us waves
Booming sounds on the bridge keep human
civilization awake
The fishing boats are beyond this century, they
are evening fireflies

Sometimes I hear the azaan, or folk songs in the
billowing waves
Which bank are you on, Neera, I'm in the middle of
the river

My arms know quite well how to swim, my legs too
are the oars of a barge
Drifting all the way from Phuleswar
It's low tide now, a counter current
There's no sky, only a downward pull from
bottomless night
Who will go in search of the delta, my body seeks
the desired arrow
What kind of tree are you standing beneath, Neera?
On which ivory veranda is the end of your sari
Heaven's flag?
The moon near your navel and golden boughs on
your breasts
Show yourself, answer, sorceress
Which bank are you on, Neera, I am in
the middle of the river

TAKE THIS TOUCH

Take this touch and all else is silence
Torn pages flutter away, unwritten pages too
The cascade from the snow peak has everything
    except a torrent of sounds
Take this touch and all else is silence

Sparrows bring in dawn, the cuckoo sleeps, and
    the cedar wood is awake
Beauty's crown slips off the dew from the blueness
Take this touch and all else is silence

The sun moves on, have you not heard a
    mistaken childish cry?
Death beckons this side and on the other
    immortality is sternly silent
'Remember?' The call is so old, memories
    are washed away in centuries-old water
What water? Whose? An ancient warm flow
Take this touch and all else is silence

I WISH

As if it's easy to be lost this way
To mingle with the crowd as a beggar
Whirling like this from heaven to clay earth
A lifetime as a man, living with the name of man

Man lives in beauty, and so, seeking the solution
to the riddle of colours in a woman
    makes the optic nerves
ache where the eyebrows meet, trapping longing
My lifespan, my obsession for plucking flowers
The water flows from river to sea, from sea to sky
I yearn so much to return to the
    grip of love

WOMAN

Atheists do not believe in you, woman
Spreading your hair out like an archway
you are the enemy of the revolution
You are actually invisible to many eyes
So many haven't even heard your name
Just like, mixed into the water, a
watercolour light

They know lovers or sisters
Mothers or wives
The girls peddling milk, or those who
sing and dance
sweat in kitchens
stretch out bony arms holding babies at crossroads
go to schools of sadness in frocks or saris
add their tears to the mason's cement
collect donations for charity with a tin

take the tiller his stale rice when the sun turns cruel
With a novel near their head,
nap in the afternoon
All of them are fine
Everyone knows them in repose, in their bodies
On days of joy or sorrow
A brief companion

But woman? Where is she?
The one with whom hordes of burnt-out poets
have been besotted
Where is she? Where is she?
Spreading her hair out like an archway
where is she standing?

How anonymous you remain in this crowd
Just like, mixed into the water, a
    watercolour light

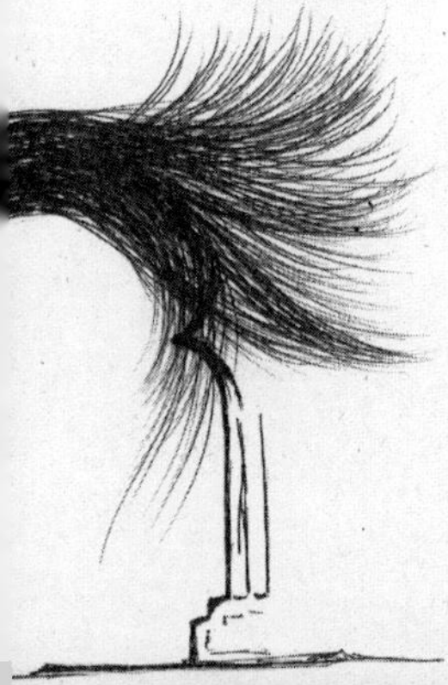

BLINDFOLD

Arundhati, my everything,
open your mouth, kiss my tongue, let the universe
    and hell hear
Arundhati, be the light, light things up, light, light,
Arundhati, light –
Not the torchlight in the eye, the light in the breast,
    Arundhati, won't you
stand like a lighthouse?

Feet on breasts, a pair of fluorescent thighs
I am reminded of the beauty of
fish on temple walls – why so much beauty? Is it the
    food of those born blind,
A red rag to a bull
Chanting to the sun immersed in water, like
    blindfolded love
Arundhati, all life, take my eyes, my breast
Take my lips, pluck out whatever you want

Pluck them out, blight them, crush or scatter, throw
    away, Arundhati

If you give me love, Arundhati, stabbing poetry in
    the back I will
die with it on the pyre, that will be best, toss one eye
    into the water
I so wanted to go to heaven, bury my face, breasts
    don't cast such a shade
Anywhere, not in the woods on earth,
    not in drawn lines
Or in the elation of flesh
Unconcealed faces are so busy, so veined, rushing
from one end to the other as in a trance, in revenge,
in space, in ruination
I too return from unlove, Arundhati, to drink the
    tears from your eyes
When I see the earth, heaven, College Street,
    set on fire

I too whip art, destroy it, kick it to hell
Your body is art, my body is art, Arundhati yours
and mine

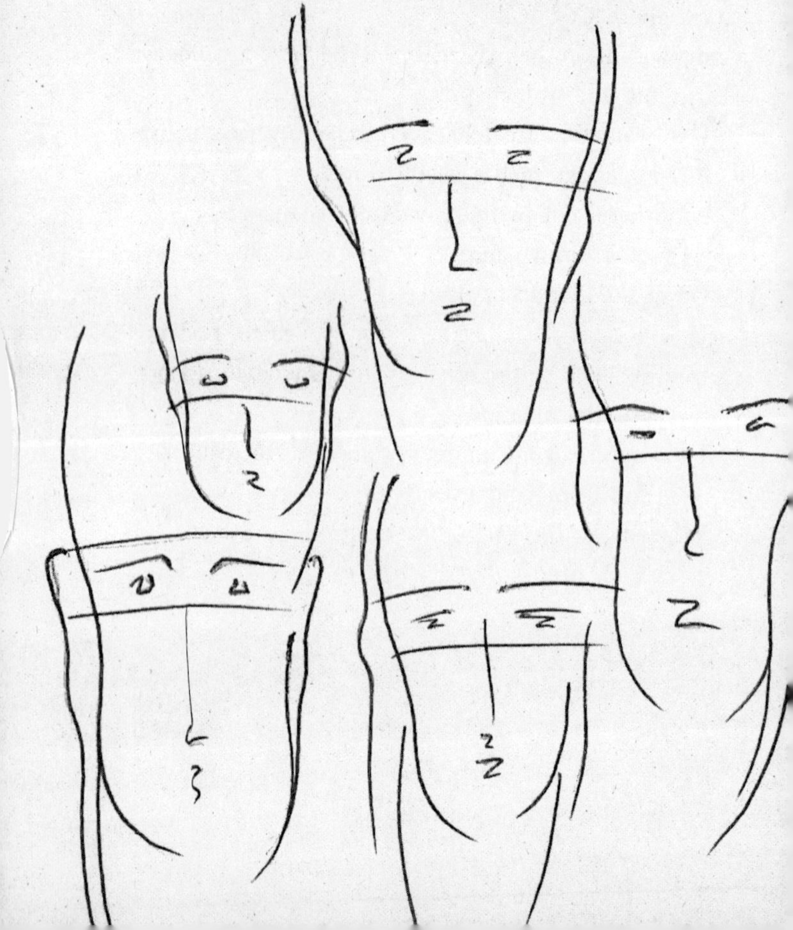

DON'T YOU REMEMBER?

For now there's world peace, an hour and twenty-
    four minutes
Throwing a sharp blue beam
An alien bird flew off
Keep sitting, lower your eyes

A red umbrella by the quiet chair,
    slippers near the door
The sun on your hand plays on the sea of your face

Let my myself go to Central Asia for some time
I'm no one, I'm a parched holy man
Raise your right hand,
    set off fireworks with your finger
Everyone knows I'm a flame-eater,
    you can easily give me
    all the gunpowder from the war
Keep sitting, lower your eyes
Near you soles the sky, like a carpet

Love is nothing, there are other terrible times for it
Heavy pillars all around, in their crevices
the nests of sparrows
I have seen much kindness, seen the mockery of
death
So many clouds, so many clouds,
life is wrapped around
symbolic clouds

A flash of lightning, listen, an hour and twenty-four
minutes
A flag, white, brings the god of the eye
All else stilled, merged in the light and dark
Keep sitting, lower your eyes
We're meeting after a long time, do you remember
nothing, Neera?

BENEATH THE BOKUL

Wait beneath the bokul tree at five in the evening
I'll be there for sure, I'll see you
What if I don't, what if I can't?
What if the devil reaches up from hell to grab my
    feet?
The bokul bough has shed a momentary flower
Who is dragging me backward by a fistful of my
    hair?
Which people set fire to buses and trams at this
    precise moment?
The wind is wistful at the scent of bokul, there's a
    whisper in it
Each and every leaf is watching you in anticipation
You remained standing alone
A small watch with a black band on your fair-
    skinned right wrist
Nothing else, your loneliness in the middle of this
    scene
No bokul tree anywhere in the world
    will ever forgive me

EASY

How easily I would make a million flowers bloom
Or light a few suns, moons and stars
On a whim I would blow out the moonlight
(Remember which?) and put out the sun (remember
    that too?)

Critics will point at me and say things,
    don't believe them
They might call me a child, or dull, or
a peddler of magic – torn tent, cracked music, in a
patched black shirt what a game of death
he is playing in the poor girl's eyes
The audience laughs, unimpressed; only the poor
    unthinking girl
suffers from an illusion of sickness;
    don't believe them

Look, you critics, how easily I hold the three worlds
with the little finger of my left hand

Darkness, ocean, mountain,
all stare at me in astonishment
Only you people have forgotten the language of wonder
Come to my house, you'll see how bizarre it is,
The roof above, look around you,
I haven't used walls
You will always live within walls with dreams and phlegm
See how the different winds move about my house
like loyal servants, dusting the parapets on the roof
Day and night busily try brushstrokes of different shades
In the room without walls I paint on the girl's eyes
So much easier – the image on the eye than in the world outside

It's you people who are the dull children,
go back, critics
Don't believe them, girl,
if they call me a peddler of magic

NEERA'S AMUSEMENT

When Neera is hurt, I am exiled for seven lifetimes
I cannot bear it, cannot, cannot, how do others
bear it?
All those people on the road with wan faces, don't
they have a Neera?
Have you had to be bankrupt through this lifetime,
sad pickpocket?
Alas Writers' Building, alas Lalbazar, none of you
had a chance to know Neera
How crude your lifestyle, how ruthless your self-
oblivion
When I take up arms, Neera shields this
green earth
Sometimes I say impatiently,
Life isn't just a childish game of love, little girl
Neera answers with mild amusement, besides the
childish game of love
All else is pooh!

WEB OF ILLUSION

After a year and a half you raised your eyes for a
glance
How did you make me so bereft of desire, Neera
A rectangular table between footprints of transient
light
How did you make me so bereft of desire, Neera
I smell incense in the illusion of your face, like
pictures on a Persian carpet
Laughter interrupted on a casual evening, mutually
separated by two yards,
How did you make me so bereft of desire, Neera

Doors closed and windows open, or is it the other
way round?
People pass by. 'When did you return from your trip
abroad, Sunil?'
Your eyebrows meet at my answer, amorous in tiny
spectacles,

Or perhaps pictures don't favour all kinds of glass
Secretly I take back the small gift I brought you
How did you make me so bereft of desire, Neera
Just for those eyes, did I run all this way just for a
 glimpse of those eyes?

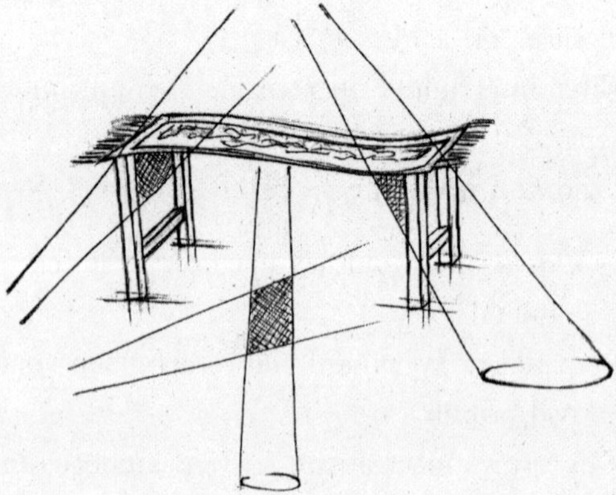

FRAGMENT

The sleep, the sleep-canopied face, of the one I love
 is so unfamiliar
Who is the one lying next to her? Where is he?
The body is another matter, even the loose hair,
 sweat on the eyebrows
Are the body, the silent restlessness on the feet, and
 the warmth of thighs
Still when she turns on her side, fists half clenched,
 magic on her lips
This life is incomplete, love is a fictitious bumble-bee
Or without metaphor, the dim bathroom light, no
 one woke up
Insects of the night dash against the closed
 windowpanes, making a sound
She is lying with her hair loose, on the thin
 drawstring of her petticoat
Sleep-traveller, which kingdom are you in, whose
 travelling companion?

Have I ever told you that you're not in my dreams
Only as much as is fenced in by wakefulness, beyond
that is forbidden
Because it is only as much as is fenced in by
wakefulness, we are no one beyond it
Love is a fragment of verse,
the rest will never be written

THE WITNESS

Hand touched hand, no one saw, did they?
A robin saw
On the steps I touched her lips
No one saw, did they?
A piece of paper fluttered away

By the river, eyes locked with eyes
All sorrows were exchanged
No one else knew
Suddenly the steamer whistled

THIS EARTH KNOWS

This earth knows some hearts are empty
This earth knows some murder bees
Some are lost in desolate hours on sad dunes
This earth knows that man has still not
Come to know man

NEERA'S LAUGHTER AND HER TEARS

Far below her eyes, Neera's
tears
tremble
Her laugh spreads from the veil
of her mouth
to her breasts, arms, fingers
Her dress laughs, twirling her wet evening hair,
    Neera
gives me her laughing hand
Neera's amusement plays on the crossroads in my
    palm
The odour of the sea escapes her disguise
She glances at me, dalliance drips from Neera's
    twilight-reddened lips
With secret caresses and hidden looks I tell her
Calm down, Neera!

That bewitching smile doesn't delude me,
    I know it all
From the sound of the planet-shaking deluge
    I can feel
The warm air by your mouth
Calm down, Neera!
The birds on Neera's dress play on her
    laughing breast
Rising from her waist and hips a stream swirls
Dazzling every corner of the universe she offers
    the glint of her teeth to evening
Uncoiling like a snake she puts her fingers to her
    lips saying
Shhh!
I know
Far below her eyes Neera's tears tremble

PARTING

We meet, we talk, still I remember our parting
Vile mountains are amassed from dug-up earth
Even when you face me
    the transparent air separates us
Such is my anger,
    I think of the transparency as my enemy

The word love has been diluted greatly of late
In fact love is swept away by a flood
There, everyone can see
I do not care for such exhibitionism

The word parting is like a white pustule on the skin
Fingering it surreptitiously gives a kind of pleasure
The joy of creation,
    and yet the muffled pain of sadness
Meaning to say these words every day, Neera,
I go back instead

Only the midnight street dog gets to know
When my loneliness deepens I use the darkness
to build
your replica
How easy it is to hold this replica to my breast
How close the embrace

The French kiss holds the long-lost taste of
    adolescence on the river bank
In the first rain
Don't you see that image in your bathroom mirror,
    Neera?

YOU ARE THE TEMPLE OF TIME, NEERA

The bluish tinge on the moon, that's where Neera's
    mournfulness sticks
It's nothing much, the moon can be blown away
    with a muff
Just like seasonal changes in the ocean, like
A letter from exile
Neera said goodbye to someone with her hand on
    the edge of the forest
The sound of rain on the end of her sari, leaves and
    vines in her dancing eyebrows
She's so far away
The green wilderness sinks into the yellow darkness
How will I go there, how will I find Neera?

You live in a circle of words, strict metres
Befit you, free verse, if you like I can even deal

you a blow with my breath, far easier
If you even dismiss the reach of the pen, Neera,
and go to the temple of time to play as its
pealing bell, if you mingle in the green of the
laughing water of the river, it is so much further
than distance, a magic wand near your navel
What trick is this, magician woman, what drollery
with me in it have you brought blindfolded into the
maze?

TOUCHING NEERA'S SORROW

This distance? It's nothing. Crossing a thousand
    light-years
In a flash I kneel in front of you
Before my warm breath touches your naked waist
I want to draw your feet
    hidden by the embroidered edge
to my breast
And wet them with kisses and tears
My thirty seven-year-old heart trembles
Thirty-seven years of my life in the world becomes
    a lie
Tears after ages, this forgotten word
Appears so tender
I wish I could mix my sorrows with yours
    to caress you
Ripping apart the social fabric of behaviour
A moment swells
I leap out of my chair and at your feet...

Too much noise outside, atmospheric low-pressure
Serial humour in the destruction and seeds of creation
and harvest
Multitudes of people sweat according to their own
patterns
That's the finest time – when all this is irrelevant
When a man returns to the unsatisfied staircase of
his personal paradise
When the bee imprisoned in the body is reminded of
childhood memories like cardamom smells
The borders of the sky are rebuffed by your
spirited pride
I wait for the tilt of the neck that can sway the past,
present and future
My heart trembles
I don't speak
If the ocean of pain can be touched by touching
breast to breasts

I rise from my chair, crossing the impossible distance
My eyes are dry, but still, before kissing your feet
I yearn to shed tears

NEERA, GAUTAMA BUDDHA

They're killing scores in Punjab every day
But at midnight I only want to write
a hymn to Neera
Kirpans and gun-barrels sprout around Neera's face
Two sets of sighs, the death-bringers and the dead,
sear the breeze
The ink dries in my nib, I look for another pen
all over
as a bolt of blue lightning races
from one end of the sky to the other
Gautama Buddha's eyes flash for a moment
At once the drone of a squadron of planes tells me
armed flights are on their way
to every region on the border
I cannot find a pen, cannot find the matches,
in the eclipsed moon,
Neera's face is lost

Merchants of darkness wake up, the city sinks to hell
My head on a pillow, gazing at the face of worn
civilization
I give Gautama Buddha the right – once, just once –
to kiss Neera's mouth
Let the two of them hold up the victory-flag for a
few moments at least
With this thought I grasp sleep like a bolster

GOT THE BLUES

Got the blues
Got the blues
Got the blues
No one knows
It's a secret
Not on my face
My eyes are open
Though they're closed
No one has noticed
Day after day
The days pass by
In hope, in hope
In hope in hope in hope in hope
And now my lips
Cannot taste
The tastes they love
Not even woman
Not even woman
Not even woman

Not even wine, not even words
Got the blues
Got the blues
Got the blues
At sundown
On my own
On the streets
On my own on the streets on the streets
Seeking nothing
Going nowhere
Wanting no one
Seeking nothing going nowhere
I'm a man too
All I have
Or all I had
All I have or all I had
In the flower
In the seed
In the worm
Like flames like flames like flames and flames

Got the blues
Got the blues
Got the blues
Still they pass
The days just pass
In hope in hope
In hope in hope in hope in hope

AGE

So am I growing older? I ask myself, laughing,
several times in the bathroom before my shower
Even a pirouette or two in such severe solitude
    can do no harm –
Should I exercise to slim down, wear tight trousers?
Out of breath with laughter in the evening
I tell Neera,
Have you been told I'm growing older?
    It's in the papers.
It's true – my chest hair, sideburns, stubble,
    are all greying
Here, see for yourself
Everyone will say, what do you mean young,
    he's old
This magic can't be cracked –
    how a young man can age
But still people always grow old and die

I'll die too
Having loved some more, written some more poems
Surely I'll die too
Isn't that right?
What is this place I've wandered into, so unfamiliar
My kingdom was huge, but beyond that the body's
infinite music gives me pangs even to lower my eyes
I enjoyed this journey, saw not a few sights, after all,
Even the darkness is sweet.
    Give me your hand, Neera,
I want its fragrance

Only near you, I think, Neera, has time stopped
    flowing, even now.

DO NOT PUNISH ME

Do not punish me, why is there so much blue water
by your head
A misunderstanding must have caused the storm in
the evening sky
Do not punish me, why did you leave with the book
incomplete
So much noise, a strange silence hangs from the
mountain range
Black tents against the sky, all the wretched of the
earth lie there
Only one of them outside; lift his loneliness like the
neck of a swan
Do not punish me, Neera, give me the warmth of
adolescent love
All my life I
Crave indulgence like an unruly child

AFTER EXHAUSTION

Raising my lips from your mouth I gaze at your face
You didn't keep a single one of your promises
Were you supposed to have wept this way, to have
looked at me like this,
    crinkling the corners of your eyes?
Beneath the clock at twilight,
    were you supposed to have
arched your body in play like a cat at my kisses?
Now the wind makes a sound like a river
I came to tell you three words in your lips
In your eyes I saw black magic
Now I feel no sadness, no rage, no envy
Now you can scatter the flower ornaments from
    your body
to the wind, let someone protect you
On days of sorrow you broke your stern vow
Drowning the river sound, two drums thundered
    like clouds

It's time for some plain-speaking, girl, none of us
Knows whether we will live two years more – or five
My words plummet to earth like birds in a cold land
I've got a letter written in the vowel endings of
hieroglyphics
A pillar of water breaks through the ice suddenly
When I bury my face in your breasts and sniff them
When the tree finds its soul, without support in the
wind
The sunflower
will bloom very late today, an orange light burns in
the green room
My blood is sceptical, both forms of intoxication felt
good this evening
Shifting my tired head I've trained my eyes
on your cheeks
Open your body to another, why did you tempt me
I said nothing, you didn't keep your word,
hurt and saddened

I found it hard to breathe,
tears sprang to my eyes too
The eyes know this only too well
I sank into doubt

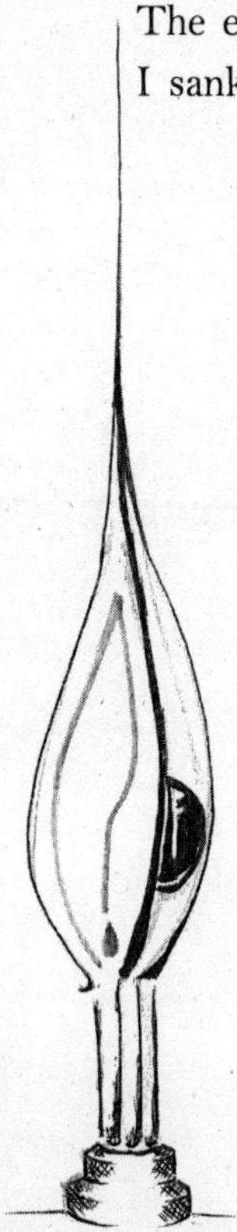

LOVELESS

I gave the last of my love to the woman before you
Now my heart is bare, like boulevards of the night
The hard asphalt glitters, bedecked in lights,
    still I know
At every turn anticipation lurks in the darkness,
    forever
This street will stay adorned, no one will come,
    desolate, loveless
I gave the last of my love to the woman before you

Your beauty makes me forget others,
    who can find a match
for your loveliness? No one's so foolish,
    they look away,
Look away, who can save me from sparks passing
    between eyes
I'm not bold enough to say, go back, go

I am without love, go back, go,
The oak is so greedy for the sap of the body like
roots
Don't expose that exquisite grace of your frame
Turn your eyes away, turn your eyes away
When you put your hand on the desk and lean
forward
Your breasts are visible, in them, like desire
The glow of sunshine,
an array of flowers on your breasts
Blood clots in both my eyes beneath my brow
Which god will you worship
with these blood-spattered flowers?
Look away, look away, the enemy is
standing in front, executioner brows,
turn your eyes away
Your beauty makes me faint with desire,
still in loveless attraction I wish to dress you
like the arbour, still on a loveless body and eyes

I want to draw rivers clouds forests,
    still a loveless life
has made my lose my love far too prematurely
Now my heart is bare, like boulevards of the night

DON'T BE LOST, NEERA

Ours were times of a new life every day
The light in the sky like a shard of glass
On hesitant footsteps from the horizon, like a woman
    living away from home
You came forward
Covered with white swan feathers, a chain of flowers
    around your throat
I was afraid

It was no time for homecoming, most were going
    into exile
The city was burning in violence then, men plunging
    their daggers
Into other men's hearts

Religion roasted its food on the fire from burning
    corpses on the road
Vomiting patriotism like bloodstained phlegm

A prisoner in the attic, I didn't recognize you
Then I leapt down with a small notebook into
A dense blueness

You stood on the bridge in Dakshineswar
The river in your eyes
The desolation of deep night over the city,
  bells pealing
From all the schools…

Our were times of a new life every day
I remember, like a cavewoman you suddenly tore off
  childhood
Hugging and kissing the tender crimson winter sun
  at dawn
The kadam tree in Hari Ghosh Street was shedding
  diamond fragments then
The first pointed tram of the day passed, saying,
  wake up, wake up,
Afternoon, midnight, and evening all mixed up, like
  a revolving stage,

I was screaming my lungs out in processions, bleeding
through the nose
Hunger licking like flames everywhere
Oh that magical, beggarly appetite, like Yayati's
An entrails-twisting hunger, like in the lowest
chamber of hell
With each blink of an eye I saw frantic mother-
figures on the balcony
Their eyes like birds'
Our dream was that every single mother in the
world would one day
Serve steaming rice to their tiny children
Bullets and explosions on College Street
You got off the bus,
and at once began the gunpowder festival
Began in the same bus
Someone raced away and leapt over the park railing,
falling like a pole
Burying his face in the grass

Our were times of a new life every day
You were a woman, you became Neera
Putting on a moustache, I played a clerk at a medical
warehouse
My shoestraps torn, I squat in front of a cobbler
on the road
No one recognizes me, behind my back everyone's a
stranger
Sometimes I am the cobbler, and they, the pedestrians
Sometimes I am the road, people walking over
my breast
Sometimes I am the silence, or the restless roar
You gave a coin to the blind old man, the clock at
Sealdah Station stopped
All the people rushing out of the train came to a
sudden halt for a few moments
And then the arson began with ringing sounds
The police weeping from teargas fumes, the Chinese
not acknowledging our brotherhood

The impact of pamphlets flung several people into
potholes on the road
Twisting their ankles
Three living puppies rolled about joyfully in the
drain
A group of white men with red hair used their
French cameras
to photograph them
You sat alone in the examination hall, no question
papers came
I stooped, looking for the coins that had slipped out
of my torn pocket
At the festival of flowers you let the end of your sari
wave like a flag
I lay next to the crematorium all evening.

Ours were times of a new life every day
The lustre of the body fell on every magic scene
The body peeped into poetry, sometimes a shadow
Sometimes the disobedience of flesh and blood

Sinking now and then,
    appearing for a tête-à-tête at others
Kalidas's hornet touched your quivering lips
Turning into water weeds,
    I put my tongue in your navel
Like Modigliani's women the moonlight glitters on
    your fleshy thighs
By turn I am a baby and you, the eternal mother
And you are a little girl,
    whom a tyrannical king wants
The ocean flings a gigantic wave at the sky
The heavens descend to the underworld
A tantric sniffs the flower in the vagina
Unsatisfied, Mahamay says, more, more
Oh, that sport, that unveiling of hearts
The history of copulation on a springtime bed was
    written
Sitting by the window without clothes, arms around
    each other

At twilight or at dawn
A cigarette in my hand, a comb of gold in yours
The forgotten world returns little by little, in space
A soft voice
At twilight or at dawn, droplets of water iridescent
    with seven colours
You gazed at them,
    there was no plane in the sky now
Harmonizing with Keats,
    you chided Newton absent-mindedly
At that moment I was reborn

We realize our mistakes, Neera, once again we build
    small rooms of sadness with sand
We are still frolicking like naked children
    on the seashore
Shielded perfectly at times, the century's casuarinas
I cannot see you, for you I have dipped my pen
    in the inkpot

I did not touch you,
like a pregnant doe you disappeared in the hills
Each successive storm
is blowing the horizon further away
As soon as the magic wand is waved, bolts of
lightning from heaven
are planted in the earth
Everything is wordplay, turning of pages
I snatch glances at the gooseberry in my hands, it
looks at me too
And twinkles a smile
You're alone in the farthest boat, Neera, you have
unfurled your wings
In the speeding mail train I cannot read the name of
a single station
From the factional politics of the school committee,
you moved away behind the door
I am spending a series of afternoons in a chair in a
room with glass walls

And yet so much shade beneath so many trees by the
    river lies unoccupied
Those who had said the revolution was here are
    writing their memoirs
And those who have been wiped out have been
    wiped out far too permanently
The cameras of the men with red hair are still
    roaming about the nooks and crannies of bylanes
No one talks of love anymore
Human civilization bursts into laughter on hearing
    of love
One or two people weep by themselves in the
    bathroom, splashing water on themselves
We have to go much further, Neera,
    don't be lost to me
We have many lifetimes left, don't be lost to me
Neera, nectar-child, don't be lost to me

NO ONE KEPT THEIR WORD

No one kept their word, thirty-three years have
passed, no one has
In childhood a wandering minstrel had suddenly
stopped and said
she would sing the rest of the song three nights
before the full moon
So many dark nights have eaten up the moon since
then but she never came.
For twenty-five years I've waited.

Nader Ali, the boatman at my grandfather's house,
had said, grow up
I will take you to see the lake at Tinprahar
On a lotus you will see a snake and a bee playing
How much more do I have to grow up, Nader Ali?
Must my head

pierce the ceiling of this room and touch the sky
before you take me to see the lake at Tinprahar?

I never managed to buy a single Royal lozenge
the gloating Laskar boys would suck on their
lollipops
Like a beggar I stood at the Chowdhurys' gate to
peep at the Rasa festivities
Amidst a constant stream of colour, fair-skinned
women in golden bangles
laughed in different pleasures
They never spared me a glance
My father had touched my shoulder, saying, one day
we'll also...
He's blind now, we never got to see anything
No one will return to me
the Royal lozenges, the lollypops, the Rasa festivities

Tucking a scented hanky into her breast,
Baruna had said
The day you love me truly
My breast will also be just as fragrant
For love I took my life into my hands
Wrapped a red rag around a wild bull's eyes
Scoured the universe to bring back 108 blue lotuses
Still Baruna didn't keep her word, her breasts only smell of flesh now
She is still just any woman
No one kept their word, thirty-three years have passed, no one does

ANOTHER MAN

The one who writes is not me
Why must you hold me responsible?
Have I bitten through the chain like an angry
leopard?
His childhood was spent on river banks
He has seen the hidden cracks in families
Searched for his mirror in fleshy water, shattered it
But I went to school, reading on public roads
I found a whip, becoming, in the emptiness
A horseman

The one who writes is not me
The one who writes is not me
He is now in Neera's company on a mountain peak
Even beats the wind with his clever phrases when it
comes to turbulence

He has no shame in becoming a beggar
So much frenzy in him for destruction
He is not afraid even to kill an embassy official
Do you think he ever stays slumped like me
Face buried on my desk?

NEERA AND ZERO HOUR

I'm not sick anymore, now to recover from the illness
And wait for the next one. Near my head now there is no window,
a pair of windows across my breast, only dry eyes
rest on the wall, like a cold compress on the brow
The chilled hand has retreated, on this terrible morning
I have no need to rise, I stay in bed, ten-thirty comes and goes

Out of these essays and belles-lettres, translations, the novel begun
five years ago, the diluted prose for newspapers
I want to rise, smashing my way through everything
At ten-thirty – blinded eyes, short hair – tearing apart the ironed clothes

And chains on my hands I am now in front of your
house, Neera, spitting on the ground I say
I will destroy this palace one day! In this palace
lives pan-Indian injustice. The monarchy will begin
here afresh. I
have heard the solemn sound beneath the bridge,
one day
profane success must be plucked out at the roots

Small sorrows in verse, I have gone back many times
and seen that my new poems begin this way
Neera, I gifted you
a coloured bar of soap
For the last time
my soap will wander over your body
across the breasts, near the navel, in affection
It will caress you through enigmatic laughter
Wear away, and want that your body
should not be immortal...

Intolerable! Flinging my pen away
    I go off to the distant sea,
swimming in the dark with sharks' babies
When I return I'm sleepy, across the table two
    women
Like little girls, like Tatars seeking blue or Negros
    seeking god
I am hurt and angry, the clear sounds of rage,
my tea-flavoured politeness turning yellow!

I am now with a friend at Saha-babu's shop, now
an injection given to my friend makes me suffer, now
I beg for a hirsute frown on the veteran poet's
    comely face
On my knees, my fury and lamentation
    touch the ceiling
Before returning to the floor,
    now at a foreigner's party
I am a youngster from Faridpur, my ugly feet caked
    in mud

Mingled with greed for decent clothes, I remove my
    teeth to show
the ugly white-skinned woman my epiglottis,
    no one here
knows of the pain in my lower body. Before dinner
White and McDavid fly into space
    in a 14-minute film
Insane! Insane! A slice of the world away,
From a rope of gold
Someone hangs, but I have got thc poetry
Straightaway, 9, 8, 7, 6, 5… counting down to zero
Mismatched time is silent, turning around,
    this is outer space,
watching the explosion of a thousand stars
Was Oppenheimer the first to count backwards,
    quoting the Geeta?
Some people climb into emptiness, others descend
    into it, for the first time
my fears of death and immortality are dispelled,
    with a smile I worship

Om Shanti. Oh roots of recent countdown arithmetic,
You are blessed, you are passion, you are Neera, you are my personal salvation.
Today I am worthy of being saved by the world.

NEERA EARLY IN THE MORNING

A man's shirt above her petticoat,
    Neera early in the morning
Her face framed by loose hair
    that's forgotten the comb
The scent of waking on her lips,
    untouched by toothpaste
Her hands unadorned, her earlobes unburdened
Opening the window, you let a flash of wind bathe
    you

Neera without make-up took me far away at dawn
    suddenly

I met you for the first time a million years ago
The river was named the Saraswati, or was it
    nameless
The tree, too, was like silk-cotton or rosewood
Twilight ringed with fire in its shade

The bark of the tree had circled half the body,
Dust or pollen in the hair,
    a greedy bumblebee hovered
with the hope of drinking nectar from your lips
Stealing Kalidas's metaphor, perhaps it's pardonable
You hurled a bolt of lightning
    with a twitch of your brows
At that moment the rain came,
    taking off your garments
you entered the river, the river was naked too
Three wild swans kept swaying with the current

Our forest interlude, its memory,
    hasn't dulled a bit, see?

My pelvis covered with leaves, I stood close by
Holding a club, Valmiki had not yet
uttered his couplet after the heron was killed
I had no language, but still I was blinded briefly
by the lustre of beauty, throwing down my weapon

on the ground I put my arms around nature
And kissed her so, as though it was you, you, Neera
Diamonds, rubies, gold and silver under the earth…

Now you'll go to the bathroom, a different picture
all day, all needs are needless

MORTAL

Sometimes I feel, Neera, as though you're even more
distant than my birthday
You walk alone in the forest where leaves have been
shed
The sound of leaves crunching
beneath your silken feet
On the horizon the mountain, like a buffalo's shoulder,
has blended
The sun set behind it, its victory cymbals crashing
All of this seems more distant than my birthday

Sometimes, looking at the sky reveals the death
of a star
A shiver runs through the heart
The eyes descend on nature, on earth
At these moments, Neera, I feel

Like waging war against mortality
wedging the flag of heaven into your brown fist
announcing to the world that the miraculous light
on your chin will stay
frozen there forever

Then I can see, in the distant forest where leaves
    have been shed,
your enigmatic smile
You know that white pigeons play in the evening
    sky
They wipe out the darkness too, like a glow in the
    eye – and on earth
So much sadness
Man's sorrows outlive his lifetime

A SILENCE HAD WANTED

A silence had wanted – to touch another stillness
They went in opposite directions
Never even met in this lifetime
Life remained on the land washed by sun and rain
And the river close by
A shy girl, come to fetch water
    sees a dead swan, its neck twisted
Sadness spreads from surprised eyes to fingertips
The moonlight celebrates suddenly with war drums
Why? There's no meaning to it
The way the vibgyor brows of the handsome sun
climb to the forest peak in the rain
And nearby, the honey-hunter suddenly breathes in
    the tiger's stench

A silence had wanted – to touch another stillness
They went in opposite directions
Never even met in this lifetime

NOT A LIE

The essence of poetry is truth, and yet aren't poets
 blatant liars?

I have often slung a necklace of metaphors around
 Neera's neck
At dawn
I put in her palms
Dew-soaked white flowers
The petals are like magic apparatus
They know how to disappear suddenly
It's been so long since I touched flowers, cigarettes
 burn my fingers now

I am a dandy in perfect clothes
While the evening breeze flutters
I am rapt in arguments and pleasures with friends
The same I at midnight, my poetry notebook open,
 am a solitary traveller by the desolate river
My hands begging for beauty shorn of logic

On one or two rare days, my beggarly ways
turns even Neera partly compassionate
Like piety on a pilgrimage, grace touches me
Piety on a pilgrimage? No more or no less?
I haven't seen a single jewel-encrusted throne in my
    lifetime
Still I lay out a diamond-studded throne
    for Neera
If she ever comes, she won't sit on it
But only place on it
a foot moist with water

Not a lie
You must know, Neera, that's how it's bedecked

THAT EVENING

I received my seven hundred and fifty-first joy the
day the clouds appeared in the evening
leaning over
the rose garden
and the annoying thorn penetrated your foot
The air was overwhelmed, the sky
held a tired, darkening light
There was no hubbub of colours
No inhibition
Such a fountain of laughter from such tiny lips
The scene could outshine temple sculptures

Then the rain came, bringing seven hundred and
fifty-two
Cherry-coloured hands, the contours of the chin
Eyes locked

Every breath fragrant with rose, the kind that
 should be preserved with care
Such magic, the wind speeds towards nine hundred
 and forty-nine
Naked nature has never been so close, I think
The secret god is vanquished by the living thorn
A thousand images of beauty, or of joy, in one body?

FEVER IS WONDERFUL, STAY IN BED, NEERA

You've been in bed three days, Neera, disturbed
sleep in your eyes
Transparent butterflies all over your fevered
bedclothes, the ceiling, beneath your bed
A chill outside the mosquito-net, the sound of a
waterfall in the bathroom
Curled up underneath a maroon bed sheet, the
sunlight doodling only on your feet
Fever is wonderful, stay in bed, Neera, don't eat
apples
Nor grapes or pomegranate, it's not a hospital after
all, in your own bed
don't eat any of these, don't read a book, darling
girl, keep your eyes open
Tell the doctor with a light smile to take a break and
fly off to Kathmandu

You were far away for a long time, today you're so
near, as though we're meeting in space
Space? This pomp of desolation swimming up in the
blueness
This unseen, dazzling, imminent attraction of art, so
many images written
Don't you sense on your body, Neera, someone's
healing breath?

THIS WINTER

I have promised, I must visit once
the other side of lost this winter
Where the heart of the water is in flames
Where the wind has etched tenderness on stone

Now, in summer, a thick veil of harshness
Emptiness reigns in fullness everywhere
Roads that took a dip in the river
have shaken off the droplets in the sun

This winter, beyond the home and forest
Rinsing off the fatigue and the grime
Where the unknown makes its own solitude
I have promised, I must visit once

SCATTERED THOUGHTS

1

I really don't care for hell. I want to return to heaven.

2

The best place on earth is Dhalbhumgarh. He who has not been there is not a complete man.

3

Touch a woman's most restless spot, tongue it, and the world trembles
Not my world, not that woman's world, the unreal universe

Witnessing this sight under a completely dark moon
    is a lot like
tasting death without dying

4

It is true that many of us have slept many nights in
    crematoriums.

5

A blind beggar on Zachariah Street offers immortality for one paisa. Those who need immortality can pay him a visit.

6

All sorrows are not sacred, all dreams are not for telling others, all roads do not lead to Rome, all love is not for women, not every white sheet of paper wants to be sullied, all windows cannot be opened, not all poets are treacherous.

YOU STAND ALONE, NOT QUITE ALONE

In a half-dark cantilevered balcony, Neera,
you stand alone, not quite alone
Fireflies twinkling, secret eyes, small desires
Large waves and small waves, of wind or the sea
break down mountains of sand, pleasant valleys
You stand alone, not exactly alone
So many warm breaths around your body
Who called? Not the moon, if you look away,
on this side is pure mortality, the end of civilization,
Raging flames on the other.
    The body on fire in its pores
The blazing comet slicing through the belly of the
    sky
The narration of silence,
    the exchange of storms between
breasts is invisible, from one death begins

Another long journey, Neera, you stand alone
in silence, not quite alone, darkness at noon
The disguised troubadour has found a mirage
somewhere
Beauty rinses her mouth with both hands, duty,
wealth, lust
at her feet, solitary woman, you do not sense the
touch of
a failed lover on your chin, thighs, nipples,
so very distant

NO, THERE WAS NO ONE THERE

Some love by mistake, some don't even love
Some eat the world with cunning, some just leave
without even returning

Clouds gather near the moon above,
the sheep grass on the mountain is on fire
Those meant to be living are not, the wrong people
are alive

Dreams shatter, yet, unknown women make for
more dreams
Dull, bloodstained metal, emerald or diamonds swing
At their necks

All my love is the love of the beggar, as if there's any
value to it
It's like a watering can,
promising to be present but disappearing

Like fireflies in a
thorny acacia shrub

I drink poison, thinking it is nectar, is poison so sweet? But they say it is salty
They leave me in the hands of death and go away, over and over again
They – who?
No, there was no one there

PRIDE TRUSSED BY TRUTH

One of these hands has touched Neera's face
Can I ever sin with this hand again?
On the late afternoon balcony
Her face was lit up by a recklessly bold ray of light
Like a telegram, revealing in an instant
Neera's grace
Laughter mingled with her eyes, brows – or were
    they crystal drops?
You want to call such a woman girl
I raise my right arm, tell my coarse palm
    in my head:
Be worthy, grow worthy…
I touch Neera's cleft
One of these hands has touched Neera's face
Can I sin with this hand anymore?
These lips have said to Neera, I love you
Do lies befit these lips anymore?

Going down the stairs I remembered I hadn't told
    her the most important thing
An alien wind will bear her away
    like a featherweight swan
All the stairs will be destroyed
    by a sudden earthquake
Rooted to the spot, I look at Neera's eyes…
Love is an intense promise, like a trap,
Pride trussed by truth – my eyes sting –
Standing on the stairs
These lips have said to Neera, I love you
Do lies befit these lips anymore?

ART

Art is common property, it doesn't belong to anyone
I am filled with fear at this thought, I consider this
truth my enemy

Is the woman named Neera merely a woman? My
mind is fixated
Neera's simplicity or casual pleasure
The sudden radiance in her fingers or
her early morning face
I look at these, my eyesight fails me
So familiar, so near – then why so distant
The flush of art adheres to Neera's beauty
I am frightened, my smothered sadness turns to ice

You want to stop playing girls' games and enter the
world of art, Neera?
You are the illusory jungle goddess in the symbolic
forest

Your smile holds the reflection of an Italian century
Beams of art flash in the teardrops in your eyes
Art that is pleasant but not personal
Can I possibly let you commit adultery by sleeping
    with art?
No, Neera, come back, come back to me
There is no exile for you from me or for me
    from you
Come back, come back to the circle of my arms

WOMAN AND ART

Before awakening the sleeping woman I look at her
The dispassionate slant of her neck,
    her brows like a canto
Dreams or unfinished words on her lips
Just like many women in one woman, or
    living in a mirror
A ribbon of black hair dangles on her chin
I don't want to brush it away, since time immemorial
    there have been many metaphors for braids
Her sari displaced from her breasts – slipped off,
    they would say
It happens
A blue blouse, white bra, the pink hint of nipples, a
    drop of perspiration
The smooth belly, the faint moon of a navel, her
    knotted petticoat
On her knee the fold of the fabric, the strange
    hubbub of lines

Her soles – like Lakshmi's footprints painted on the
floor
This woman

The woman and the sleeping woman
are not the same
This silent scene could be art, if I maintain
the correct distance, if my eyes are ascetic
if I hunt and gather the letters of the incantation
I don't see the woman, I present myself
Because it grows
I put out the light out of sheer politeness
Then begins giant festivities for demolishing art
Plunging my face into her lips, her thighs
I pass on the news
that does not swim away on time's currents

THE ARTIST RETURNS

The artist returns, but is this any way to go back?
Treading the river bank, where thorns abound
And jagged sandbanks nearby, where the road ends
You call this going back? This isn't a pleasure jaunt
Leaping suddenly out of a woman's arms
A tender hand on the brow,
    moistened letters on the desk
So many things still to be done, all those overtures
But he seems to know it's too late now
    to realize his mistake.

Such yearning in the heart, lips that care so much
Still he must go back, must go back
You call this going back? This isn't a pleasure jaunt
The road ends there
Whoever returns to a strange land?
    You can go. But return?
Wouldn't it have been easier to swim?
They'll all say you've made a mistake, artist
An unsatisfied, regretful, enormous mistake

FOR YOU

Neera, take the tidiness of the afternoon
Take the distance of the night
Take from me a sandalwood breeze
Take the bathed freshness of the virgin earth by the
 river
Take the scent of lime leaves in your palm
Turn your face this way, Neera, I have kept for you
The finest, most colourful sunset this year
Take from me the smile of the beggar boy on the
 road
Take the first green of the cedar leaves
Take the surprise in the green beetle's eyes
Take the whirling wind in the solitary evening
Take the tinkling of ox-bells in the forest
Take silent tears
Take the loneliness of waking up at midnight
Let fog-sprinkled night-flowering jasmines be
 showered

On your head, Neera
Let a nightbird whistle for you
If all that is beautiful is obliterated from earth
Still, darling girl, I want to leave all of this
for you